# GHOSTS OF THE JERSEY SHORE

# Ghosts of the Jersey Shore

## Lynda Lee Macken

Ghosts of the Jersey Shore
Published by: Black Cat Press
P. O. Box 1466
Point Pleasant Beach, NJ 08742
llmacken@hotmail.com

Copyright © 2011 & 2024 by Lynda Lee Macken
All rights reserved. No part of this book may be reproduced or transmitted electronically, orally, or in any other fashion without permission in writing from the publisher.

Photo Credits: Cover engraving from *Historical and Biographical Atlas of the New Jersey Coast* by Woolman & Rose (1878); pages 8, 17, 20, 31, 57, 71, 73, 79, 101, 114, 116, and 121 courtesy of the Library of Congress; p. 11, Wikimedia, Freholdman12, CC-BY-SA 4.0; p. 14, courtesy Craig Johnson; p. 40, N. Currier; p. 42, Point Pleasant Historical Society; pp. 60, and 81, Shutterstock; all other photos taken by the author.

Although the author and publisher make every effort to ensure the accuracy and completeness of information contained in this book, we assume no responsibility for errors, inaccuracies, omission or any inconsistency herein. Any slights of people, places or organizations are unintentional. For information, please contact Black Cat Press.

ISBN 978-1-7360069-8-6

Book Layout & Cover Design by Deb Tremper,
Six Penny Graphics.
www.sixpennygraphics.com

*To Astrid, Ruth and Liv.*

*For whatever we lose (like a you or a me),
It's always our self we find in the sea.*

—e. e. cummings

# CONTENTS

### INTRODUCTION — ix

### SANDY HOOK
Sandy Hook Lighthouse — 1
Joshua Huddy's Haunt — 3
Fort Hancock — 7

### PORT MONMOUTH
Seabrook Wilson House — 11

### LONG BRANCH
President James Garfield's Ghost — 17

### WEST LONG BRANCH
Shadow Lawn — 20
Guggenheim Library — 24

### ASBURY PARK
Stephen Crane House — 27
Paramount Theater — 30

**SPRING LAKE**
The Essex Sussex Hotel — 37

**POINT PLEASANT**
The Shore House Tavern — 40

**BAY HEAD**
The Grenville Hotel — 44

**LONG BEACH ISLAND**
Barnegat Light Beach — 50
Barnegat Lighthouse — 53
Mansion of Health — 55
Phantom Schooner — 59
Surflight Theatre — 61

**ATLANTIC CITY**
Absecon Lighthouse — 65
Resorts Casino Hotel — 70

**MARGATE CITY**
Lucy the Elephant — 76

**OCEAN CITY**
Flanders Hotel — 79

### NORTH WILDWOOD
Hereford Inlet Lighthouse — 83

### WILDWOOD
J. Thompson Baker House — 88
George F. Boyer Museum — 91

### CAPE MAY
Congress Hall — 94
Inn of Cape May — 100
Hotel Macomber — 104
Cape May Fish Market — 107
Emlen Physick Estate — 113

### CAPE MAY POINT
World War II Bunker — 116
Cape May Lighthouse — 119

Acknowledgements — 123

Bibliography — 124

Websites — 127

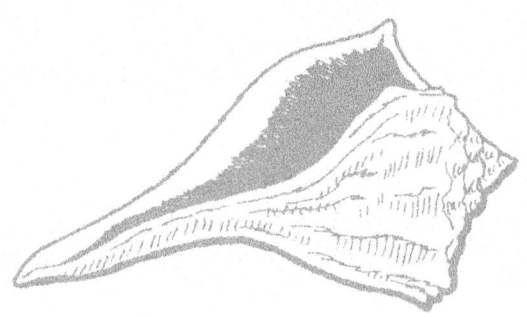

# INTRODUCTION

The history of the Jersey Shore teems with tales of pirates and privateers, rumrunners and wreckers. Pages of New Jersey's past abound with subversive stories but the frightening fables pale in comparison to the seaside phantoms and shipwrecked specters haunting the state's coastline.

The Jersey Shore is prime real estate for ghosts for a number of reasons. Many incorporeal spirits possess unfinished business. Plenty of the following stories involve premature deaths, which might explain why some ghosts do not realize they are dead.

Moreover, quartz crystals enhance communication and the composition of New Jersey beach sand is 90% quartz. This mineral absorbs electromagnetism and heightens sound enabling the recording of spirit voices, known in ghost hunting circles as electronic voice phenomenon (EVP).

The human body is comprised of electrical

energy and during times of extreme stress or trauma, this electromagnetic force discharges into the atmosphere. The energy lodges in physical structures and even furnishings. The embedded energy enables psychics to read the room or the object (a process called psychometry) thereby offering glimpses into the past.

Oftentimes refurbishing old buildings wakes up the sleeping energy causing the spirits of the dead to come back to life, so to speak. This type of lingering spirit is a residual haunting and could explain the presence of ghosts at Monmouth University in West Long Branch. There are even some haunted buildings constructed over old structures where there is an accumulation of leftover energies such as in Cape May's Congress Hall.

Though no one can fully explain or predict the appearance of an unearthly presence another natural force enhances contact with the unseen world—water. Water attracts electromagnetism and combined these two elements create a unique energetic environment. The atmosphere inside structures along its path can become highly charged such as Absecon Lighthouse in Atlantic City.

The powerful blend of electromagnetism and water can produce a rare effect on our perceptual senses *but not all the time*—herein lies the mystery… Sometimes approaching a haunted site with the *intent* of connecting with the supernatural can coax the spirits to open up and offer a peek at times past.

Enjoy a hair-raising adventure along New Jersey's shoreline. Explore the environs of the coastal ghosts who populate the places they loved or where they breathed their last briny breath.

# SANDY HOOK

## SANDY HOOK LIGHTHOUSE
### 84 MERCER ROAD

Sandy Hook is a narrow spit of land that comprises part of the Gateway National Park Recreation Area. The site is home to the Sandy Hook Lighthouse. Constructed in 1764, the oldest standing lighthouse in the United States is still operational. The unique octagonal design ensured stability during severe storms. Near the tower is a brick, three-story keeper's quarters complete with veranda and two chimneys.

In 1850 a skeleton was unearthed sitting at a table in a secret underground passage beneath the keeper's house. Nearly a century later, the corpses of four men and one woman were found buried at the base of the lighthouse.

Some visitors claim to feel an ethereal tap on their shoulder when wandering about the site. Is the tapping ghost a displaced spirit seeking attention? Possibly, it's a lost soul looking to find their way home.

# JOSHUA HUDDY'S HAUNT

During the American Revolution, and well into the 20th century, military installations existed on Sandy Hook. Today the barrier spit is part of the Gateway National Park Recreation Area. When the sun goes down on the peninsula, some say Captain Joshua Huddy's spirit roams the shoreline in an eternal search for his executioners—and with good reason.

The Highlands region played an important role in the Revolutionary War. Strategically important for both the British and Colonial armies, the area was constantly trafficked by troops from both sides.

Joshua Huddy served as a member of the Monmouth County Continental Militia. He actively, and successfully, pursued Tory gangs who plundered the region in search of American rebels. Huddy received a commission to operate a gunboat, *The Black Snake*, as a privateer in August 1780. Captured at his home in Colts Neck on September 1st of that year, the raiders attempted to burn down his house, but Huddy surrendered instead. His captors tried to transport him across the bay to New York City, then British territory, but patriots on shore fired at the boat. The vessel capsized and Huddy escaped by swimming to safety despite receiving a bullet wound to the thigh. This incident infuriated the Loyalists and Huddy became a marked man.

On March 24, 1782, the enemy re-captured Huddy, this time during a raid of the blockhouse he commanded at the Toms River (then called Dover) salt works. Huddy thought he'd be exchanged for a Loyalist prisoner but when his captors received word that a Monmouth County Tory named Philip White had been killed, William Franklin, the last English royal governor of New Jersey, and Bejamin Franklin's son, ordered Huddy's execution in retaliation. The Loyalists claimed Huddy's complicity in White's death even though they held him in captivity at the time.

Initially, Huddy was taken to a sugar house prison in New York City then transferred in irons to a guard ship at Sandy Hook where he was held until his execution on April 12, 1782. On that date, a party of Tories took him to the Highlands' Gravelly Point where he hanged. A party of patriots came upon their fallen comrade and carried him to the Old Tennent Church for burial in an unmarked grave. (A stone to his memory now exists next to the church, although the exact location of his burial remains unknown).

When Joshua Huddy's spirit manifests on the Sandy Hook shoreline he strides toward visitors as if to assess their hand in his death. When assured of their innocence his apparition turns and walks away eventually fading from view.

A monument to Captain Huddy is also installed at his namesake park at Bay and Waterwitch Avenues in the Highlands to commemorate the spot where he hanged.

# FORT HANCOCK

During the American Revolution and well into the 20th century, military installations existed on Sandy Hook. Numerous fortifications stood at the north end of the six-mile peninsula protecting New York's harbor from invasion.

In 1899, Fort Hancock was established on the site and thirty-four buildings were erected in support of the organization. An elegant row of Georgian Revival style officers' homes still stand sentry at the water's edge.

Several years earlier Battery Potter was constructed and outfitted with the nation's first and only steam-lift gun battery, the most sophisticated weaponry to date. The wide variety of weapons installed at Fort Hancock range from cannons to Nike missiles.

Even though many of the gun emplacements and structures are disintegrating a tour of the complex offers an enlightening experience and can elicit a ghost story or two.

A chilling tale concerns a volunteer who made up a bed in the old barracks Building 102. After he smoothed the covers an impression appeared on the bed as if someone lay there. He straightened the bedclothes again and left the room. Returning only moments later, the indentation was again visible.

When the volunteer shared this incident with other workers he discovered they experienced similar strangeness. The volunteers concurred the bedridden revenant could possibly be an ordnance accident victim from the weapons facility.

History House is a restored home open to the public on Officer's Row. Several years ago a park volunteer spent the night inside the old house. During the night she awoke to loud footsteps coming up the stairs. She got up to investigate but found no one. The steps resounded later on and this time they stopped at the foot of her bed. The woman chilled to the bone when a strange voice asked if she wanted some juice.

A visitor touring the house was once a resident in the dwelling next door. She claimed an officer committed suicide by hanging himself inside the home and alleged his ghost appeared to her regularly when she lived there as a child. Previous families fled when they witnessed the dead man's spectral head floating in mid-air and a pair of disembodied shoes walking up the stairs. The tourist said the officer's ghost liked the woman's family so he toned down his scary antics and allowed them to stay.

For many years, a spectral soldier bearing arms stood at attention on the porch of Building 20 (20 Hartshorne Drive). The New Jersey Audubon Society now occupies the structure but reports no haunting activity.

# PORT MONMOUTH
## SEABROOK WILSON HOUSE
### 719 PORT MONMOUTH ROAD

*US News & World Report* named the 1663 Seabrook Wilson House one of the three most haunted houses in America. Well protected behind the dunes of Sandy Hook Bay, the 17th-century structure is the oldest house on New Jersey's shoreline.

During colonial days the British believed someone in the house spied on their naval operations. This is how the one-time tavern earned the moniker Spy House. The real spy however peered from nearby Garrett's Hill. The house survived the Revolution by operating as an inn. When the British left their ships to wind down at the tavern, the colonists successfully plundered their undermanned vessels by sneaking up to the ships in whaleboats.

Since the 1950s, over thirty separate ghosts have been identified at the Spy House and hundreds of spirit sightings have been documented. According to a township employee, the ghostly population includes, "Abigail and Peter, Lydia and Reverend Wilson, Captain Morgan, Robert..."

Loud sobs emanate from a bedroom where Abigail stares out the window waiting for her husband lost at sea. Gertrude Neidlinger saved the historical dwelling from the wrecking ball and founded the Shoal Harbor Museum at the site, functioning as its curator. She felt Abigail's son Peter randomly switched on tape recorders positioned throughout the house that explained its history.

Psychics perceived former owner Reverend William Wilson perform a funeral service in front of a bedroom fireplace. They also sensed men strategizing in front of the first floor fireplace.

In his epic tome *GHOSTS, True Encounters with the World Beyond,* Hans Holzer states that on July 4, 1975 a group of local boys were in the blue and white bedroom upstairs when suddenly the sewing machine door opened by itself and the foot pedals starting pumping without benefit of human feet!

One evening as a volunteer left the building,

he witnessed children playing on the grounds. He watched for a few moments and realized their clothing looked unusual. Their outfits denoted an earlier era; their provincial garb a dead giveaway to their ghostly identity. Since then people sit for hours in the parking lot waiting for a phantom to put in an appearance.

Thomas Whitlock, the first permanent white resident of New Jersey, built the house as a one-room cabin. His spirit, on a few occasions, tagged along with visitors and actually went home with some of them. An employee shared that Whitlock likes attention and once she inadvertently brought him home with her. "He drove my dog crazy," she said.

From time to time, the aroma of Whitlock's pipe tobacco wafts through the air. He may also be the culprit who steals workers cigarette packs. "He always puts them back though."

At one time pirates commandeered the house led by the bloodthirsty Captain Morgan. The brutal buccaneer despoiled women and murdered children. Youngsters visiting the museum observed his faceless phantom dressed in a long, dark hooded robe at the top of the stairs and his terrifying bearded reflection in an upstairs mirror.

During one of the many séances conducted at the house, psychic Jane Doherty contacted a spirit named Robert who claimed to be Captain Morgan's first mate. Robert revealed the existence of hidden tunnels leading from the house to the harbor. Sonar readings substantiated the possibility of tunnels.

Her psychic impression revealed the presence of a trapdoor used during the Revolution by George Washington when he frequented the inn.

Indeed a trapdoor stood right where the psychic predicted and history substantiates Washington's stay at a church across the bay in South Amboy.

Approaching the house, a visitor slammed on his brakes certain he ran over a little girl. Fortunately the sight turned out to be an apparition. Historic records reveal a young girl named Katie lived in a nearby house. She died in an accident after being run over by a horse drawn wagon.

The Seabrook Wilson House is part of Bayshore Waterfront park. The location affords beautiful views, including Manhattan's skyline. Dare to experience the possibility of the paranormal by parking at dusk and tuning in to the spirits… Perhaps phantom children wearing old-fashioned togs will be romping through the yard.

The house is open to the public from April through October from 1–4 p.m. on Sundays only.

# LONG BRANCH
## PRESIDENT JAMES GARFIELD'S GHOST

In the late 1700s, Long Branch was a popular resort where health seekers, actors, business leaders and a sporting crowd frequented the grand hotels or elaborate summer cottages. Called the Monte Carlo of America, by the 1800s some of our nation's greatest dignitaries, including Mary Todd Lincoln, gathered here. By the first half of the 20$^{th}$ century, seven presidents vacationed in Long Branch as well.

Presidents Chester A. Arthur, James Garfield, Ulysses S. Grant, Rutherford B. Hayes, Benjamin Harrison, William McKinley and Woodrow Wilson all attended services at the Church of the Presidents. The church is the only remaining structure in Long Branch associated with any of the seven presidents who vacationed in the seaside resort during its Gilded Age. Moreover, it holds the rare distinction of being the only building associated with all seven of them.

The church stands at 1260 Ocean Avenue

across the street from the cottage that once stood on the grounds of the Elberon Hotel, where President James Garfield succumbed to an assassin's bullet.

The wounded president arrived in Long Branch hoping the sea air and tranquility might assist his recovery from the bullet lodged in his spine. He died ten weeks later on September 19, 1881, exactly two months before his 50th birthday.

According to Charles A. Stansfield Jr., in the days following Garfield's death, his unmistakable phantom strolled along Ocean Avenue, particularly near Lincoln (!) Avenue. Like many Washingtonians of his day, Garfield delighted in happier times spent in the seaside town. For a while, he continued his evening constitutional, his spectral appearances diminishing over the years—but not entirely…

# WEST LONG BRANCH
## SHADOW LAWN
### CEDAR AND NORWOOD AVENUES

**M**onmouth University is one of the most haunted colleges in the nation. Its 138-acre campus encompasses two grand estates—Wilson Hall, formerly called Shadow Lawn, and the Guggenheim Cottage.

Woodrow Wilson considered Shadow Lawn his summer White House and conducted his re-election campaign from the estate. He utilized the enormous porches as a speaking platform to address the crowds assembled on the grassy expanse.

In 1918, Hubert Templeton Parsons, president of the F.W. Woolworth Company, purchased the property. Snubbed by American society, Parson's tenancy turned out to be troubled, to say the least.

A devastating fire destroyed the lavish home in 1927. Immediately Parsons arranged to construct a new, fireproof manse. Modeled after the Palace of Versailles, the new dwelling contained

130 rooms and ranks among the top twenty mansions in America.

In addition to the main hall, the elaborate estate included a 10-room superintendent house, two-story estate garage, eight greenhouses, horse barn, cattle barn, poultry house, two-story palm house, bullpen, ram pen, sheep pens, pheasant pens, rabbit hutches, an icehouse, three workmen cottages and kennels for the six police dogs turned loose on the grounds every midnight. The self-sustaining enclave maintained a staff of 100.

Hubert, his wife Maysie and her sister Bertha led a lonely existence in their sumptuous home. They were considered socially inept and despite constant invitations to attend lavish dinner parties, their old-moneyed neighbors gave the nouveau riche Parsons the cold-shoulder.

The 1929 stock market crash signaled the descent of Parson's fortune. Ten years later, the house went up for public auction. West Long Branch Borough, the sole bidder, purchased the estate for $100.

These days disembodied footsteps and pipe organ music still echo throughout the main campus building baffling all who discern the mysterious sounds. Staffers working late at night hear undistinguishable conversations and the sounds of doors opening and closing when they are alone in the historic hall—or are they?

Most astonishing is a photo taken in the dining room sometime in the 1990s. The picture captured two transparent women dressed in maid uniforms tending to a modern day dinner party. Perhaps they stayed behind waiting for dinner guests to finally arrive.

In the Office of Special Events, an unseen presence sends chills up the spines of all the workers. According to the documentary, *Shadows of Shadow Lawn*, this eerie visit only occurs during times when the office is working on a major event. Perhaps Mrs. Parson's spirit likes to participate in planning the well-attended parties thrown these days in her earthly abode.

# GUGGENHEIM LIBRARY
## 400 CEDAR AVENUE

Across Cedar Avenue from Shadow Lawn is the Murry and Leonie Guggenheim Library built where New Jersey's only vice-president, Garret A. Hobart, once lived.

In 1903, Murry and Leonie Guggenheim appointed architects Carrere and Hastings, designers of the New York Public Library, to create a summer residence. The Beaux Arts building received the Gold Medal from the American Institute of Architects.

Murry Guggenheim died in 1939 but Leonie continued to summer at her West Long Branch mansion until she passed away twenty years later. Many say Leonie's spirit glides along the grand staircase every night—her filmy, phantom appearance witnessed by mystified campus police officers. The spirit's presence on the stairs may explain the detectible creaking often heard as well as the perceptible drop in temperature.

Campus police even detected a female form wearing a white gown standing at a window in the middle of the night when they were certain the building was secure.

Many discern a definite presence that evokes unease among the library stacks. A sensitive French student became so distracted from her studies she had to leave the reading room because she felt certain an incorporeal entity observed her.

The computer room is located in a space once used as a lavatory. Several anomalies disturb this spot. Cursors move on computer screens when no operators are near the monitors; sometimes, inexplicable tiny triangles show up on the screens. Technical types cannot fathom this unexplainable anomaly. From time to time, the scent of perfume is noticeable in the space even though the workers wear no cologne.

Most astoundingly, filmmakers inadvertently captured an awesome anomaly when filming the grounds for *Shadows of Shadow Lawn*. A garden statue, who some claim to be a likeness of Leonie Guggenheim, appears to blink and crack a slight smile. Expert analysis cannot explain the uncanny movement—to see the film is to believe it.

# ASBURY PARK
## STEPHEN CRANE HOUSE
### 508 4TH AVENUE

Stephen Crane, author of The Red Badge of Courage and other works, lived with his family at 508 Fourth Avenue for nine years. The home is now a museum, performance, and entertainment venue hosting readings, plays and classic movies.

Stephen Crane (1871–1900) was born in Newark, the youngest of fourteen children. In 1883, Crane's mother purchased "Arbutus Cottage" and enrolled her son in the Asbury Park Public School system where he wrote his first short story. Much later, Crane went on to work as a journalist, filing stories from Asbury Park for a New York newspaper.

He spent his last summer at the Jersey shore in 1892 when he traveled to New York City. Three years later his masterwork, *The Red Badge of Courage*, was published to great acclaim in America and Europe.

At the age of 28, he died in Germany and his

remains were buried in Hillside, New Jersey. Unfortunately, his Newark birthplace was torn down decades ago, and the Stephen Crane House is the only remaining residence of the famous author.

Many deaths occurred in the house and ghostly claims run rampant. Sightings of people in period clothing who suddenly vanish include a female apparition in the attic window and a man in Victorian clothing was seen on the second floor. Objects move in full view of witnesses, disembodied voices and sudden drops in room temperature are reported. Astoundingly, a fireplace shovel once flew off its rack and hit a young boy in the head.

The SyFy Channel's *GhostHunters* team investigated the paranormal claims. The team tried hard but could neither prove nor disprove the claims.

So is the Crane house haunted? Some say yes… but no one can say no.

# PARAMOUNT THEATER
## 1300 OCEAN AVENUE

On September 8, 1934, the *SS Morro Castle* ran aground en route from Havana, Cuba, to New York City. One hundred and thirty-seven passengers and crew lost their lives.

During the voyage, the *Morro Castle*'s captain, Robert Willmott, died suddenly from a heart attack, Chief Officer William Warms replaced Wilmott at the helm as a strong Nor'easter developed. To make matters worse, at 3:00 AM, a fire broke out in a storage locker and quickly accelerated and engulfed the ship in flames. The fire burned through electrical cables and plunged the ocean liner into darkness. The storm drove the disabled vessel closer to shore as desperate passengers and crew tried to escape the blaze and choking fumes. The few lifeboats that were launched carried mostly crew members to safety; passengers were forced to leap into the churning ocean. An assortment of watercraft in the area assisted survivors to shore.

Unable to sail under her own power, a Coast Guard cutter eventually attempted to tow the damaged ship to its original destination. Tumultuous seas snapped the tow lines, and the burning hulk came to rest on a sandbar in front of Asbury Park's Convention Hall.

The hull still smoldered the following morning when inspectors boarded the ship in search of victims and valuables. The massive fire consumed the decks and gutted the cabins. Corpses were taken to the Paramount Theatre and were laid out on stage for identification purposes. For a small fee, interested ghouls could gawk at the cadavers. Thousands of curious spectators and reporters lined the boardwalk to see the charred remains.

The *Morro Castle* remained on the sandbar for many months and spurred an economic boom for Asbury Park since suffering the effects of the Great Depression. City officials capitalized on the event and turned the wreck into a tourist attraction by charging $5 to ride the breeches buoy onto the deck. On March 14, 1935, the ruined *Morro Castle* finally ended up in New York's Gravesend Bay for scrap.

Coincidentally, at almost the identical location off Asbury Park, the immigrant ship *New Era* wrecked in dense fog on November 13, 1854.

Asbury Park's Paramount Theatre is co-located with Convention Hall on the boardwalk. The completion of the third Madison Square Garden in New York and Atlantic City's new Convention

Center put city officials under pressure to construct a similar venue for Asbury Park.

In 1927, a mysterious fire destroyed the 5th Avenue Arcade on the boardwalk. Shortly thereafter, a referendum passed to construct a conference center on the plot. The architectural design included a 1600-seat theatre and a 3200-seat convention hall connected by an enclosed grand concourse.

Walter Reade, who owned four theatres in Asbury Park, received a contract to book movies at the venue. Since he brokered with the Paramount film distributor he named the showplace the Paramount Theatre. On New Year's Day, 1930, the film *Wings* inaugurated the new cinema which featured a mix of movies and live performances. A more spectacular grand opening followed on July 11, 1930, attended by Hollywood luminaries Carole Lombard, Fredric March, Ginger Rogers, Ed Wynn, and the Marx Brothers, among others.

When Garden State Ghost Hunters (GSGHS) investigated the infamous theatre, every team member heard inexplicable footfalls, knocking noises and ethereal voices. A few felt phantom touches. Crew member Tina Bates experienced an unseen entity pull one of her earrings off and several witnesses watched it sail across the room. The group discerned shadow people on stage and one of their thermal cameras picked up the heat signature of human buttocks on one of the theater seats.

Team members scrambled when a light bulb flew off a shelf four feet away in response to their question, *"Are you unhappy with us being here?"* Are these fuming entities leftover energies from the awful *Morro Castle* disaster? Are the incorporeal beings present here resentful over their untimely death on a pleasure cruise coupled with the further insult of morbid opportunists profiting from their death?

Several psychics sensed a fire once raged through the performers' dressing rooms and indeed singe marks still exist on the walls. Sadly, no emergency exit door regulations were in place at the time, so the entertainers were trapped and perished in the flames. When psychic medium Barbara Lee first visited the location, she received an immediate rush of information regarding the catastrophe. The space is unusually charged with a thick, heavy energy. In fact, Lee detected spirits gasping for air—hardly able to breathe, the empath perceived people suffocating from smoke inhalation.

When GSGHS captured evidence of a human form with their infrared equipment, they forwarded the video to Syfy channel's *Fact or Faked, Paranormal Files*. The program follows a team of investigators, led by a former FBI agent, who reviews various photographs and videos of alleged paranormal activity. If a particular piece of evidence warrants further investigation, the team sets out to recreate and explain the sighting.

In this instance, specialists recreated the anomaly but determined GSGHS' choice of equipment was erroneous. However, when *Fact or Faked* cast members performed their own investigation of the historic theatre, they corroborated many of GSGHS' above mentioned findings, thereby authenticating paranormal activity at the theater.

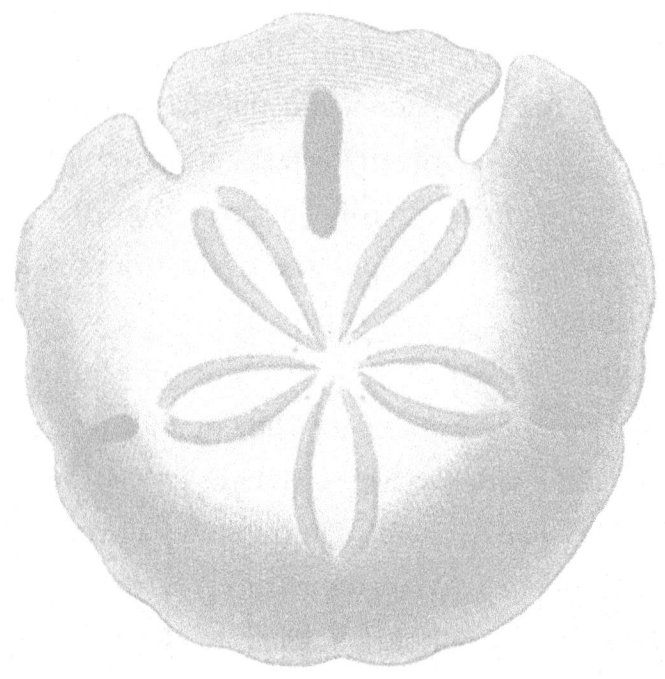

# SPRING LAKE
## THE ESSEX SUSSEX HOTEL
### 700 OCEAN AVENUE

The Essex and Sussex seaside hotel endured as a magical milieu amid wind-swept beaches and a beautiful spring-fed lake. Opened in 1920, for decades thereafter the hotel reigned as the crown jewel of the Jersey Shore attracting royalty, presidents, and the elite. In 1981, the venue appeared in *Ragtime*, providing the perfect backdrop for the 1900s high society film. Today the edifice is a luxury condominium complex.

When the massive building stood vacant, a lone security guard insured the building's security and warded off trespassers. Sometimes in the dead of the night, the caretaker discerned the din of revelers in the ballroom. Music, laughter and the clamor of people partying filtered through the cavernous structure. When the caretaker reached the room and opened the door the noise stopped and the room stood empty.

Workers refurbishing the building for condominiums in 1982 felt certain they were watched by unseen presences. They avoided working on the fifth floor because there they glimpsed a dark shadow peering at them from the end of the long hallway. When they tried to see who watched them the furtive shade darted out of sight.

Author Charles A. Stansfield, Jr. reports another resident wraith at the oceanfront hotel is the ghost of a long-time resident who lived at the old hotel. The wealthy matriarch so enjoyed her residence that she does not want to leave. She habitually frequented the lounge for a nightcap every evening. On occasion, her beautifully attired apparition is spotted gliding down the elegant main staircase. Don't look twice—you'll miss her.

*"'Wreck of the Ship John Minturn,' (Captain Stark) on the coast of New Jersey in the terrible gale of February 15th. 1846, 3 o'clock a.m. with 51 persons on board." By Currier & Ives.*

# POINT PLEASANT
## THE SHORE HOUSE TAVERN
### 2114 ROUTE 88

On February 15, 1846, a severe storm caused a number of shipwrecks along the northeast coast that shocked the nation.[1] One of these was the *John Minturn*, a three-masted packet ship bound for New York from New Orleans.

The *Minturn* made it all the way to Sandy Hook, but the storm blew the ship southward and out to sea. Captain Dudley Stark tried to run the ship aground near Mantoloking to save passengers and crew, but ran into a sandbar. Ultimately, 38 people from the *John Minturn* perished that day.

The Shore House Tavern is housed in a building that at one time operated as a hotel. At the time of the wreck, a stagecoach stop stood on the site. On that awful day, the structure served as a temporary morgue for victims of the shipwreck.

Some say Captain Stark's spirit resides in the tavern and stomps about the second floor. The

---
[1] The 1846 wrecks sparked the creation of the United States Life-Saving Service to assist shipwrecked crews and passengers.

unnerving noises are attributed to residual psychic debris recorded on the ethers from the long ago tragedy.

*At the time of the disaster, a stagecoach stop stood on the site of the Shore House Tavern. The structure served as a temporary morgue for victims of the John Minturn shipwreck.*

When the tavern functioned as Magee's West Side Tavern, some alleged the spirit of an eight-year-old boy lingered in the dining area and even enjoyed karaoke. Patrons swore they heard his disembodied voice singing along to songs.

Servers, bartenders and patrons witnessed dishes smashing, spooky silhouettes, and Captain Stark's full-bodied apparition. Boxes flew, lights flickered, and a former employee recalled the basement door mysteriously slammed behind her one night.

A former owner viewed the tales of ghosts and hauntings with a grain of salt and even greeted the ghosts when opening and closing the bar. When he removed a broken chair from the attic, a psychic informed him that the spirit wanted their chair back. The psychic possessed no prior knowledge of the incident, and the tavern owner swiftly returned the chair to its original place.

The haunted eatery was featured in an episode of the *Jenny Jones Show*, and ghost hunters often visit. When paranormal investigators inspected the upper floor with digital cameras, audio equipment and electromagnetic testing devices, they found evidence of a spectral presence only in the corner where the chair was positioned.

Not surprisingly, orbs of light, thought to be spirit energy, showed up in the photos taken in the attic as well.

# BAY HEAD

## THE GRENVILLE HOTEL
345 MAIN AVENUE

The historic Grenville Hotel is situated on Barnegat Bay Island, one block west of the Atlantic Ocean.

The historic hotel is a relic of days gone by. In 1890, Anna Nunemaker bought the property and commissioned Wycoff Applegate to build the structure. In 1922, the hotel was sold to Nellie Georgette who renamed the guesthouse the Georgette Hotel.

When fire destroyed the nearby Grenville Arms, the Georgette was re-named The Grenville.

Over the decades, The Grenville has been home to several owners and has hosted thousands of guests. From the amount of paranormal activity reported at the site, it's evident the hotel still holds the energies of the past. Many feel the resident wraiths are the spirits of the hotel's former owners continuing from beyond the grave to welcome guests. The hotel's proximity to the ocean is an additional ingredient enhancing the recipe for ghosts on the menu here.

The most dramatic ghostly manifestations reported are apparitions of guests dressed in Gilded Age finery. The spirits appear oblivious to the mortal world, absorbed as they are in another dimension. Other oddities that occur at the hotel are cutlery and dishes moving on their own, and the sound of disembodied footsteps echoing in vacant rooms, particularly on the third floor.

As one guest watched TV in Room 304, she heard children laughing in the room next door although no children were currently registered at the hotel. During the night, she awoke from a dead sleep to the sound of someone walking in her room. The footsteps approached her bed, and she soon felt the sensation of someone sitting on the mattress! Later in the night, a female apparition dressed in a white, 1920s' era, evening gown manifested. When the guest asked the spirit woman who she was, the vision simply vanished.

Another guest who stayed in Room 306 also heard children giggling. At midnight, the spirit of a bearded man appeared. He donned a top hat and wore a vintage tuxedo as he stood in the doorway.

Full-bodied apparitions are the rarest paranormal event. Although infrequent, this type of haunting involves a spirit's existence in a place where there's an emotional or physical connection. A spiritual presence does not necessarily signify the individual is "stuck" on the earth plane. The deceased person may desire to co-exist in both worlds, a dramatic possibility according to recent breakthroughs in quantum physics. As mindboggling as this sounds the concept is something to contemplate...

When working alone, some staffers discern disembodied footsteps walking down empty halls, and the sound of furniture being moved in empty rooms. A few get the palpable feeling of an invisible presence watching them while they work. When one employee fell asleep in the lobby, he awoke to the sounds of kids playing and witnessed their transparent spirits as well.

The spirits haunting the Grenville Hotel & Restaurant are harmless and only add to the allure of the seaside hotel which offers a classic beach vacation.

# Garden State Parkway

Millions travel the Garden State Parkway en route to their favored shore destination. Sometimes the legendary Parkway Phantom catches drivers unawares along an Ocean County stretch of the roadway.

Typically, the specter emerges on foggy nights and those who detect the tall, male ghost always describe him wearing a full-length, belted raincoat. Usually he appears to be wildly flapping his arms. Some motorists say his behavior looks as if he wants to cross the roadway. Others stopped to help the man but when they do, he vanishes.

Some feel his erratic behavior is a deliberate warning signal to motorists to slow down and be cautious of danger ahead.

One evening, this writer observed a tow truck ahead and a man on the right side of the road, his arms flailing excitedly. The tow vehicle displayed plenty of flashing lights; this man did not need to alert passing cars. Suddenly I realized I witnessed the Parkway Phantom. Perhaps a casualty himself, maybe he wants to steer others out of harm's way.

The sightings date to 1955 when parkway construction was completed. Most manifestations occur along an eight-mile length of roadway near Exit 82 close by the Toms River Barracks of the New Jersey State Police.

Law enforcement will not comment on the reports but they do admit to a larger than usual number of accidents in the area.

# LONG BEACH ISLAND
## BARNEGAT LIGHT BEACH

John Bacon, also known as "Bloody John Bacon," led a band of brutes called the Pine Robbers. Toward the end of the American Revolutionary War, the rebels secreted themselves in the Pine Barrens and preyed upon Patriots.

On October 25, 1782, a forsaken British freighter foundered in the waters of Barnegat Shoals. The skipper of the privateer brig, *Alligator*, Captain Andrew Steel, and his 25-member crew spent the better part of a day hefting the cargo from the cutter's belly. At nightfall, the exhausted men fell sound asleep on the dunes.

Unbeknownst to the sleeping seafarers, Bloody John Bacon and his raiders lay in wait on Island Beach directly across the inlet. During the day they watched the looters offload the cargo. At night, the time was ripe to reap the rewards of their furtive surveillance. The marauders massacred nearly all of the slumbering seamen, including Captain Steel; only five managed to escape the atrocious assault.

This bloody attack occurred during a truce between the United States and Great Britain as they negotiated a peace agreement. The Long Beach Island massacre caused Governor William Livingston to place a bounty of fifty pounds on Bacon's head.

In December, 1782, a gun battle involving Bacon and his men at the Cedar Bridge Tavern,[2] was the last skirmish of the American Revolution. Bacon was wounded but managed to escape.

On March 31, 1783, Captain Richard Shreve and his armed forces tracked down Bloody Bacon, bayonetted the buccaneer and then shot him, causing his death.

At Barnegat Light, a historical marker commemorates the Long Beach Island Massacre. According to legend, ghostly re-enactors replay the gory event every October. Those who've witnessed Bloody John Bacon's gray ghost brandishing a bloody saber, describe the unforgettable scene as gruesome.

---

[2] The Cedar Bridge Tavern is a historic building located in Barnegat Township. Built around 1740, it is the oldest bar in the United States. The tavern is allegedly haunted by the spirit of John Wildermuth, a former tavern owner.

# BARNEGAT LIGHTHOUSE
## 10 E 7TH STREET

Buried near the base of the lighthouse are the earthly remains of unknown shipwreck victims. The beacon's catwalk, however, harbors General Gordon Meade's ghost. Meade rose to fame on Gettysburg's battlefields but he also designed and built the Barnegat Lighthouse just prior to the Civil War. His spirit must be beaming atop the 172-foot-high tower that replaced the previous 40-foot tower ravaged by stormy seas.

In *Haunted Jersey Shore*, Charles Stansfield Jr. recounts the tale of Uncle Caleb Parker and the lucky cat of Barnegat Light.

Uncle Caleb was a lightkeeper whose skeleton was unearthed in a cellar room during construction of the second lighthouse. In front of a brick fireplace, workers found the stalwart keeper's remains sitting in a rocking chair. Laying on his lap was the carcass of a cat.

Legend says that during a particularly fierce storm, Uncle Caleb watched in horror as a schooner wrecked in the dangerous shoals of Barnegat Inlet; all on board perished.

The next morning Caleb found an unusual cat clinging to a piece of floating debris. He rescued the frightened feline and discovered the strange looking cat lacked a tail. Its front legs were shortened and its rear legs long, which caused it to hop like a bunny. He soon learned this Manx breed of cat originated in the British Isles. He also discovered she was pregnant.

As soon as the kittens were weaned, neighbors eagerly adopted the tabbies hoping one of these lucky cats would bestow good fortune to their home.

They say the cats who frequent the environs of the lighthouse today are the offspring of the original lucky cat.

# MANSION OF HEALTH

Today the Surf City Hotel, at 800 N. Long Beach Boulevard, sits on the site formerly occupied by the 1822 Mansion of Health. For years, the three-towered structure possessed the reputation as the shore's grandest hotel and the island's most haunted building.

A savage storm ransacked the Jersey Shore on April 18, 1854. The wooden packet ship *Powhatan* embarked from Rotterdam and months later drew near her New York destination. Over three hundred affluent German immigrants traveled on board the packet ship looking forward to a new life in America.

A springtime crossing of the turbulent North Atlantic is risky so Captain Myers probably breathed a sigh of relief when he observed the shore birds—a signal the schooner neared land. However, his luck, and the weather, took a turn for the worse. The ship thrashed about in the dangerous waters as gusting winds turned the ocean violent. The *Powhatan* struggled to stay afloat as a full-fledged blizzard wreaked havoc on the sea.

The wallowing ship vanquished in the violent shoals. Realizing the *Powhatan's* hopeless situation, lifesavers stood helpless on shore, sickened by the sight.

Eventually, corpses washed up all along the Jersey coastline and as far south as North Carolina Avenue beach in Atlantic City where Resorts Casino Hotel operates today. Victims were buried in mass graves at various locations including Manahawkin and Smithville. The awful carnage included mothers clutching babies in their arms and couples locked in a final embrace.

At the time, Edward Jennings was the Mansion of Health's caretaker and a designated wreck master responsible for reporting shipwrecks in the area. He went about his work piling the cadavers on the sand. The coroner inquired of any valuables. "Not a thing," Jennings tersely replied.

Months later two men found a huge pile of ransacked money belts secreted near the Mansion; a recent storm uncovered the underhanded hoard.

Although not formally charged with theft, Jennings became a ruined man. He left New Jersey in disgrace and headed south. Word eventually reached home that Jennings was murdered in a barroom brawl. Many believed justice was finally served.

The Old Mansion's clientele discovered more fashionable digs but phantom visitors found the accommodations much to their liking. For years the apparition of a woman holding a young child in her arms frequently stood at a window, shocking all who spotted the miserable wraith.

Ultimately, like many old, wooden hotels, the forsaken building burned to the ground.

The Mansion of Health may be gone, but beachcombers say the screams and cries of the doomed ship's passengers and crew are still heard on Surf City's sands.

# PHANTOM SCHOONER

A long-held, Long Beach Island legend tells of a spectral ship haunting its waters. Evidence suggests the ghostly craft is the packet ship *Powhatan* that wrecked on April 16, 1854. The ship, heavily ballasted with iron, shattered on the shoals during a fierce, late winter storm.

Centuries after the wreck and robbery, islanders are still haunted by a ghost ship which appears any time of the day or night. Not only do the shipwreck victims of the schooner *Powhatan* linger on Long Beach Island, some feel the ship itself still sails the waters off LBI, appearing as a spooky schooner.

Authors Siebold and Adams recount eye-witnesses testimonies about the sightings of a fully-rigged schooner emerging from the fog. The ship appeared to sail toward their boat at

full speed yet paradoxically kept its distance at the same time! All express a consistent scenario and convey their confusion at seeing a glorious bygone galleon, her tattered sails flapping in the breeze.

As suddenly as the ship appeared in their sights she vanished inside the haze from which she materialized.

# SURFLIGHT THEATRE
## 201 ENGLESIDE AVENUE

The Surflight Theatre is Beach Haven's summer stock showplace. Theater personnel and patrons in both the old and new theaters reportedly see the ghost of the theater's founder, Joseph P. Hayes as well as other shades.

In 1950, Joseph Hayes, and a cast of 60, breathed life into the Surflight Summer Theatre in an unwieldy 2,200-seat tent. Six years later, Hayes, donned a clown costume to introduce the Children's Theatre series at the Surflight. Also thanks to Hayes, a former garage soon became the theater's permanent residence and a costume shop went up next to the playhouse.

In 1976, Hayes suffered a fatal heart attack and a few years later the theater community founded the Joseph P. Hayes Theatre, Inc. in his memory as a nonprofit organization dedicated to raising scholarship funds.

Theaters are notoriously haunted places and

the Surflight is no exception. The scene shop is a room without windows yet despite closed doors, an icy breeze penetrates. This waft of cold air raises hackles as it preludes the appearance of a 6-foot-tall indistinct shadow. The form briefly lingers then suddenly evaporates.

Workers feel the shade, who they dub the "dark man," is the same restless spirit who frequents the Surflight's catwalk. The shadowy specter is respectful of the stage and never disrupts a live performance.

All manner of unexplained events occur in the scene and costume shops—rooms original to the old theater. Tools and costumes disappear and turn up days later in strange places.

Several years ago a chalk line, a device used to make straight lines, went missing. Workers searched all over the place to find the tool but to no avail. They gave up the hunt and went to dinner. Upon their return, the gadget rested in plain sight on top of the tool bucket.

Who is the ghostly culprit? Some think the poltergeist is an actor who used to work at the Surflight. The performer enjoyed helping out in the costume shop and possessed a reputation as a practical jokester.

Most agree, however, the Surflight is the otherworldly stage for the theater's founder. Remarkably, Hayes' spirit once showed up as a shimmering, translucent apparition.

One unforgettable summer night piano music filtered through the empty playhouse. Actors investigated the source of the music but they found no (living) body present and *no piano*. In addition to the ghostly melodies, the sound of someone tap dancing on the empty stage also baffled the players.

The grand finale is Surflight staffers and actors feel reassured the founder still looks out for his treasured showplace.

Many wooden schooners wrecked in the coastal waters off New Jersey and these tragedies earned Absecon Inlet the nickname "Graveyard Inlet." In an effort to avert further shipwrecks, the U.S. Lighthouse Service commissioned a lighthouse on Absecon Island.

Designed by General George Meade, who also drew up plans for the Barnegat Lighthouse, the Absecon Lighthouse is the third tallest masonry lighthouse in the United States. The structure rises 171 feet skyward and a 228-step circular staircase spirals up to the lantern room. The beacon towers above Atlantic City's backyard on Vermont and Pacific Avenues.

The fully restored lighthouse is listed on the New Jersey and National Historic Registries. The complex encompasses a lightkeeper's house, museum and lens exhibit.

Reports of paranormal activity date to 1905 when a light keeper observed the Jersey Devil

atop the tower. (The Jersey Devil is a mythical creature that has haunted New Jersey's Pine Barrens for over 250 years). Over the years dozens of wretched spirits gazed out from the lantern room over the choppy sea. Presumably shipwreck victims, they seem to take refuge in the light that saved so many others from a similar fate.

Another historical specter spotted on the property is that of a Revolutionary War soldier who probably perished when the *Mermaid* sank in 1779.

Since the lighthouse renovation, lighthouse visitors and staff claim dozens of inexplicable anomalies. The unexplainable scent of pipe tobacco and cigar smoke wafts throughout the premises; sounds of disembodied footsteps resound in the tower as well as the sound of the tower door opening and closing. Partial apparitions materialize; particularly an aged human hand appears at the top of the lighthouse stairs. Dimes show up in odd locations, a classic spirit apport. (Apports are gifts manifested from the non-physical to physical reality.)

The Atlantic Paranormal Society, also known

as TAPS, from the SyFy Channel's *GhostHunters* TV series conducted an investigation to assess the claims of ghosts and haunting activity.

The professional ghost hunters heard an indecipherable conversation and the sound of footsteps. As they ascended the staircase, they realized the wind caused the noises. However, video evidence showed a camera placed in the lighthouse mysteriously moved on its own and an odd light shone in the room!

Even though *GhostHunters'* evidence was minimal on the visit, the accumulated first-hand experiences override the investigators initial findings.

Take a gamble and check out this notoriously haunted spot for yourself.

# RESORTS CASINO HOTEL
## 1133 BOARDWALK

In 1850, Absecon Island resident, Dr. Jonathan Pitney, envisioned the area as an ideal place for a health retreat. The visionary brought the first railroad to the island and created today's street grid pattern. Pitney named his Atlantic City streets running parallel to the Atlantic after the oceans and the streets running east to west after the states. When the first train pulled into the station from Camden in 1854, the tourists disembarked in droves.

Real estate developers soon recognized Atlantic City's potential as a resort destination. Before Resorts International formed, two three-story wooden Quaker rooming houses, the Chalfonte House (1868) and the Haddon House (1869) stood on the site. In 1900, Henry Leeds purchased the Chalfonte House property and constructed an eight-story iron-frame and brick-face "skyscraper" which opened its doors to guests in 1904 as the Chalfonte Hotel.

The current Haddon Hall building was constructed in stages in the 1920s. The 11-story wing facing the Boardwalk was constructed first, with the 15-story center and 11-story rear wings added later in the decade. Soon after its completion Haddon Hall merged with the adjacent Chalfonte via a skyway, which still exists today.

Almost immediately ghostly rumors began to swirl. The upper floors of the thousand room hotel were freezing according to guests who felt the chilly atmosphere signaled the presence of disembodied beings. The brick and steel building swayed with the wind which howled through the halls adding to the haunted reputation.

The Chalfonte-Haddon Hall played a vital role during World War II when Atlantic City beaches were used for maneuvers and armed forces training at "Camp Boardwalk." Haddon Hall transformed into Thomas England General Hospital for wounded soldiers.

In Resorts' Ocean Tower, a feature of the original Haddon Hall and the oldest part of the property, a few people have experienced the paranormal as claimed by a hotel representative. A couple from North Carolina felt uncomfortable during their stay according to a review on tripadvisor.com. The woman wrote, *"My husband and I stayed in the Ocean Tower and the whole time we were there it felt like someone, or something was in the room with us. The sixth floor hallway just felt so creepy like someone died there. We kept hearing bumping, and the door would shake."* Thinking other guests cavorted in the hall, the female guest opened the door and found no one.

In fact several individuals did transpire there. Hundreds of soldiers billeted in the Chalfonte-Haddon Hall Hotel building during WWII and many expired from illness and their injuries. Apparitions of corpsmen walk the hallways and hotel-registration areas according to some. Could the appearance of the eerie soldiers account for the supernatural experiences reported by guests?

Former Resorts employees who used to take their smoking breaks in the basement, which served as the temporary hospital morgue, described it as "kind of creepy." Resorts claims the on-site morgue was actually on the 12th floor, but the basement location seems more logical due to cooler temperatures. Just knowing that a morgue existed on-site is enough to give one the willies!

Unlike most other hotels, Resorts designates a 13th floor. Due to superstition of something sinister associated with the number 13, it's commonplace for hotel management not to allow a 13th floor. Resorts, however, brazenly houses its Piano Bar and the Pro Bar dance club on number 13.

Curiously, another Resorts team member who is sensitive to spirits, shared that, *"As a new Resorts' employee I attended the required orientation meeting. During the course of training, the head of security took our group on a tour of the building. We rode the elevator to the 13th floor which at the time was the VIP Club. When I exited the elevator I suddenly felt surrounded by a mob of spirits—I mean a lot of spirits. It was like being in a crowd of hundreds. I couldn't understand why there were so many spirits roaming and swirling around me. We continued our tour and when finished, returned to the orientation room. Our guide told us that during World War II the hotel was used as a hospital and that the 13th floor was where the operating rooms were located. To me, that explained why there were so many spirits still wandering the corridors."*

A feral cat colony exists under the boardwalk outside Resorts. Frank Scoblete in his article "The Ghosts of Atlantic City's Resorts Hotel" published in the *Casino City Times*, states that on some early mornings, a spectral woman in black walks the beach. A multitude of mewing felines announces her arrival as her specter goes about feeding and tending to the homeless cats.

He goes on to say ethereal nurses push ghostly carriages and wheel chairs and are seen assisting phantom children outside the hotel particularly in the vicinity of the valet parking. After a while they slowly fade from view.

Think twice if you spot a Charlie Chaplin type character inside the casino. This personality is a revenant from the past so give him a nod as he tips his hat in greeting.

# MARGATE CITY
## LUCY THE ELEPHANT
### 9200 ATLANTIC AVENUE

They say elephants never forget and the haunting at Lucy the Elephant is truly memorable.

Lucy is a 65-foot-tall, elephant-shaped novelty construction built of one million pieces of wood and tin sheeting. In 1882, speculator James V. Lafferty erected the oceanfront structure in what was then called South Atlantic City to attract tourists and sell real estate.

Lafferty created a small herd of pachyderms when he raised two more ponderous structures—the Light of Asia in South Cape May and Elephant Colossus in Coney Island.

Over the years the colossal pachyderm served as a real estate office, residence, restaurant and tavern. After her last owner passed away in 1963, poor Lucy withered away and was close to extinction when kind-hearted citizens rallied to her cause and formed the Save Lucy Committee.

The 90-ton landmark moved to her present location in 1970.

The view from Lucy's *howdah*, the carriage positioned on the elephant's back, offers spectacular shoreline vistas. In pre-dawn hours, late night revelers maintain they observe a figure in the howdah enjoying a cocktail. This lone being is probably a former bartender who worked inside the elephant structure when it operated as a tavern. His habit was to relax with a drink atop the creature at the end of his shift.

# OCEAN CITY
## FLANDERS HOTEL
### 719 EAST 11TH STREET

A friendly ghost haunts the Flanders Hotel, a historic hotel located at 719 East 11th Street on the Ocean City boardwalk. This architectural gem houses the ephemeral spirit dubbed "Emily."

Artist Tony Troy painted a life-size portrait of Emily, based on descriptions from hotel staff and guests, which hangs prominently on the second floor. The brown-haired young woman is depicted standing by a piano wearing a long white dress and no shoes. Her story appears near her portrait.

Workers and guests cite swinging doors, locking doors, loosened chandelier light bulbs and the train of a white gown disappearing around the corner of a corridor as evidence Emily still happily haunts the hotel. Sightings occur near the grand piano, walking barefoot through the Hall of Mirrors and in the basement catacombs.

A gleeful ghost, Emily's spirit sings and

laughs with delight in the Flanders' many grand rooms. Even children claim they talk to the pretty woman who shares secrets with them and then mysteriously disappears.

According to legend, the unearthly Emily is allegedly the fiancée of a World War I soldier who never returned from battle. Years ago,

Emily's ghostly image developed in a photo snapped inside the hotel during a wedding.

South Jersey Ghost Research investigated the Flanders Hotel. The resident spirit provided the ghost hunters with a rich variety of psychic impressions throughout the evening. Investigators sensed *multiple* spirit energies including Emily.

Observers said the female apparition appears to be in her 20s with wavy hair and wearing a white dress. Investigators believe her real name is Marilyn or Maryann, or something similar.

Another compelling spirit is a young girl around five years of age. Perhaps a drowning victim, psychics feel she is eternally seeking her mother in the Flanders. It is possible Emily is the lost girl's mother.

Not surprisingly, South Jersey Ghost Researchers obtained physical evidence to indicate spirit activity. A large number of photos reveal balls of light thought to be spirit energy. The ghost hunters also captured dozens of EVPs and their electromagnetic field detectors displayed inexplicable readings.

# NORTH WILDWOOD

## HEREFORD INLET LIGHTHOUSE
### 111 CENTRAL AVENUE

**N**orth of Cape May, a barrier island called Five Mile Beach parallels the New Jersey mainland. Separating Five Mile Beach from the next barrier island to the north is a small gap known as Hereford Inlet that leads to the calm waters found between the mainland and the islands.

Late in the 19th century, mariners who navigated the perilous Atlantic coastline with its shifting sands and treacherous currents, needed a lifesaving aid. The Lifesaving Service selected the small fishing village of Anglesea, situated on Five Mile Beach Island near the inlet, as a site for the station overlooking the waterway. A "Notice to Mariners" announced the activation of the lighthouse on May 11, 1874.

*A man's face is evident in the window on the left. Is this the spirit of Lightkeeper John Marche looking at psychic medium Bobbi Torres standing outside? The lighthouse stood unoccupied at the time. Or was it?*

Paul J. Pelz designed the lighthouse in the Carpenter Gothic style, the only example of such design on the East Coast. The Hereford Inlet Lighthouse is similar in design to California's Point Fermin Lighthouse and East Brother Lighthouse, also designed by Pelz. The beacon boasts five fireplaces and provided comfortable accommodations for the keeper and his family.

Many vied for the coveted lighthouse position in the idyllic location. John Marche became the first keeper to occupy the distinctive seaside home. Marche served only three months before he drowned on August 9, 1874, when his boat capsized on a return trip from the mainland.

Open to the public during summer months, visitors stroll about the spectacular flower and herb garden reminiscent of those cultivated in Victorian times. Some even glimpse the former lighthouse keeper's spirit struggling in the waters of the Hereford Inlet.

During a visit to the lighthouse with Bobbi Torres, the psychic medium discerned Marche's spirit lingers in his seaside quarters. Marche committed his life to save others. In an ironic twist of fate, he drowned before he had the chance to realize his ambition. His frustrated spirit stays behind because not only did he suffer premature death, but he could not even save himself, he conveyed to the medium. The exasperated keeper feels he passed before completing his life's mission. *"No one needs saving in heaven,"* he imparted.

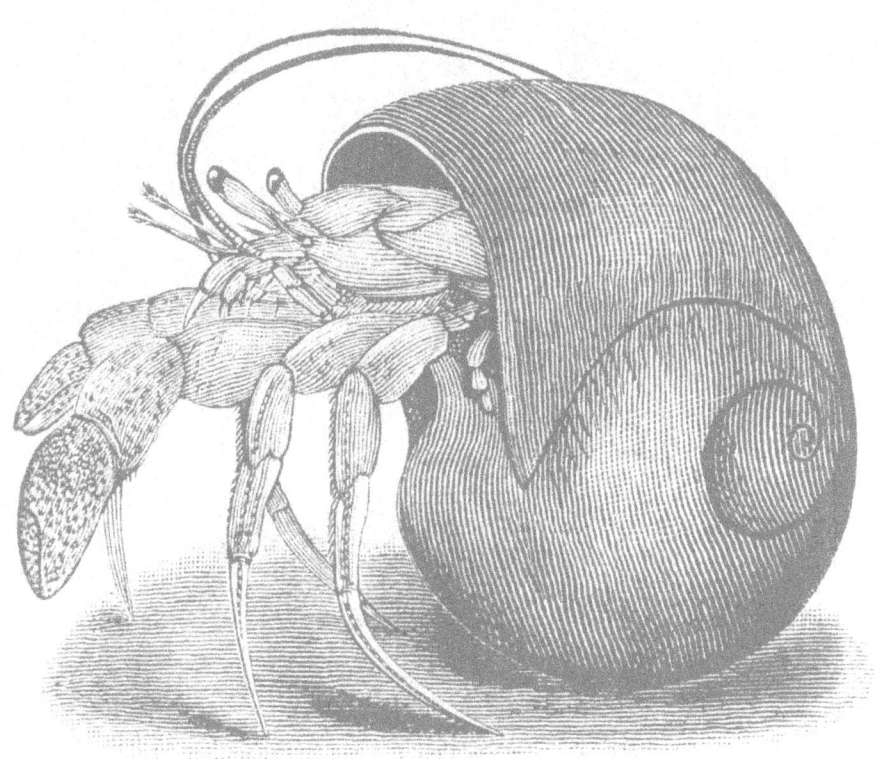

# WILDWOOD
## J. THOMPSON BAKER HOUSE
### 3008 ATLANTIC AVENUE

The J. Thompson Baker National Historic House is named after its former owner, a New Jersey congressman and founder of the Wildwoods. Built in 1904, President Woodrow Wilson stayed at the historic house during a campaign junket six days before his 1912 presidential election.

Baker served as the first Mayor of Wildwood and his former dwelling is now home to the Wildwood Civic Club. The interior décor exemplifies the lifestyle during Baker's tenancy. Period books, as well as children's toys, lie scattered throughout the house as if the inhabitants still enjoy their home. Some feel they still do.

Several civic club members avoid going into the building by themselves after dark although they can't say exactly why—*something* inside makes them feel uneasy. Some visitors to the residence heard footsteps in the foyer and on the front porch. When they looked to see who walked into the house they found no one.

The strange goings-on prompted Theresa Williams, president of the Friends of the J. Thompson Baker House, to invite the Cumberland County Paranormal research group to investigate the eerie happenings. The ghost hunters, headed by Clay Borneman, recorded electronic voice phenomena, called EVPs for short. The group taped indistinguishable voices while recording on the staircase and also captured strange noises in the attic. A journalist reporting on the paranormal investigation observed a spectral couple dressed in vintage clothing in his peripheral vision.

The civic club conducts historic house tours, a worthwhile expedition, and various other events throughout the year. Pay a visit to the home and see what appears in *your* line of vision…

# GEORGE F. BOYER MUSEUM
## 3907 PACIFIC AVENUE

The structure housing the George F. Boyer Museum originally served as Ingersoll's Funeral Home. That's sounds chilling enough, but in consequence of many unexplainable happenings transpiring in the building, the Cumberland County Paranormal organization came to investigate the anomalies.

Some of the unusual claims made by museum volunteers include unexplainable smoke scents and sweet smells. Fire was ruled out, although Wildwood has seen its share of blazes. The museum's holdings include an assortment of boardwalk memorabilia. Could the old artifacts exude an ethereal aroma of days gone by? During their inspection, the Cumberland ghost hunters caught a whiff of pipe tobacco. In every case, the smells suddenly surfaced then disappeared just as quickly.

Museum docents reported that on several occasions when they answered the ringing telephone no one was on the line. Crank caller or paranormal prankster? Also, the security alarm sounded in the middle of the night without cause. Motion sensor lights malfunctioned yet quickly returned to normal. When the motion sensor is activated, the light stays lit for a certain period before shutting off. One volunteer stated he opened the building one morning to find the motion sensor activated signaling movement inside.

The night of the paranormal investigation all of the Cumberland researchers distinctly felt they were being watched. A palpable presence gave an aura of "reserved curiosity" to quote lead investigator, Clay Borneman. He said, *"The best way to describe it is the feeling of being observed by a curious child told not to talk to strangers."* He sensed the presence kept *"peeking around corners to see what the new people were doing."*

The group captured compelling electronic voice phenomena; when asked "Do you like it here?" a garbled response was recorded. A second recording also contained indistinguishable sounds by an entity seemingly eager to communicate.

# CAPE MAY
## CONGRESS HALL
### 200 CONGRESS PLACE

The oldest seaside resort in the United States is New Jersey's *most* haunted city. There are *dozens* of haunted places nestled in the cozy enclave. So many, in fact, that entire books are in print devoted solely to the resort's undead, including this author's *Haunted Cape May* (2002).

Cape May is a national historic landmark and a treasure trove of Victorian architecture. Over 600 vintage seaside structures dating from 1800 to 1910 ornament the district of less than two miles.

Originally, called Cape Island whalers first settled the peninsula in the early 1600s and the region grew as a seaside resort long before the Revolutionary War. Travelers from the nearby cities of Baltimore, Philadelphia and Wilmington sojourned to the shore to take advantage of the cooler climate.

The locals housed and fed the visitors and

unwittingly established a new business venture—tourism. More and more people came to enjoy all the rejuvenating benefits of the sun, sea and hard sand beaches where they rode their carriages.

Thomas H. Hughes was the first to build a guesthouse for the sea-goers. In 1816, Hughes erected a three-story, rustic boardinghouse at the corner of Congress Street and Beach Drive. The first Cape May County resident elected to the legislature, Hughes officially renamed his establishment Congress Hall in 1828.

The Congress Hall that stands today is the third one to bear the name and is constructed of brick since flames devoured the prior two wooden structures.

Once known as the "Playground of Presidents," Abraham Lincoln lodged at the Mansion House in 1849 and Ulysses S. Grant and Chester A. Arthur visited Cape May in subsequent years. Congress Hall hosted Presidents Franklin Pierce, James Buchanan and Benjamin Harrison. Harrison's continual residency established the inn as his summer White House.

In 2000, the grand, L-shaped landmark underwent a $22 million historic rehabilitation, which restored the guest palace to its former 1920s-era glory.

Stepping into the grand hotel through the original 12-foot doors one can easily sense the energy of days gone by, particularly in the marble floor foyer where ocean breezes, oversized mirrors, potted palms, overhead fans and wicker furniture exude a classic seashore atmosphere. Considering thousands of guests sojourned to the site for nearly 200 years it makes sense that psychics say the structure is rife with spirits.

The basement restrooms are particularly active with restless wraiths. Both men's and women's rooms possess an invisible, yet palpable presence. The phantom's footsteps and the sound of the door are audible as the spirit exits the stall and turns the water in the sinks on and off.

After hours in Congress Hall more ethereal footsteps are perceived near the gift shops. The persistent phenomena may explain the appearance of light orbs in photos shot in the corridor.

In the *Ghosts of Cape May*, psychic medium Craig McManus wrote about his exploration of the third floor. On a dark and stormy night, McManus discerned the ghosts of two children wearing vintage bathing outfits going from room to room trying doorknobs. When the psychic asked the spectral brother and sister what they were doing they answered, "the waves ate us." (Doesn't that give you the willies?).

Although not a ghostly tale as such, the following story bears telling:

In the summer of 2002, Jack Wright left his position as an executive editor of *Men's Journal* in New York and, on a whim, took a job at Congress Hall's pool cabana. When the summer season ended he stayed behind (as dozens of the departed did!) and began writing *Tommy's Folly*, the history of the famous old hotel.

One evening Craig McManus performed a past life reading for Jack Wright. A psychic medium can use a past-life reading as a divination tool to access information about previous lifetimes. During the reading, a medium receives images or messages relating to prior life experiences, and connects with spirit guides or deceased loved ones to gain insight into an individual's soul journey.

The psychic medium channeled an astounding message from his spirit guide—*Jack Wright was Thomas Hughes in a previous lifetime!*

The reading offered a greater understanding of Wright's fondness and fascination for Congress Hall. Paranormal corroboration can be a powerful tool in discerning life's mysteries.

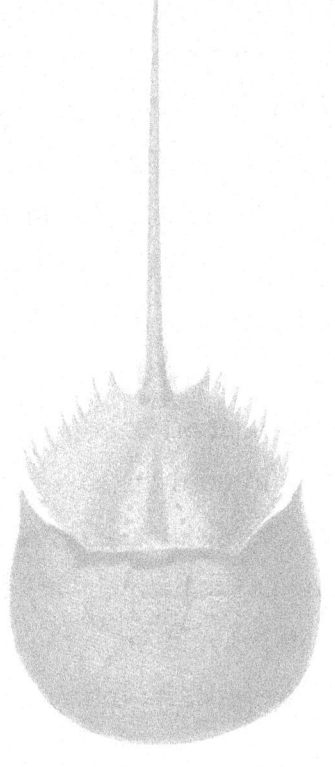

# INN OF CAPE MAY
## 7 OCEAN STREET

In the fall of 1894, contractor William H. Church began work on a 60-room boarding house on Ocean Street, a prized beachfront location. He designed the four-story structure with a French roof and roomy porches that offered unobstructed views. Called the Colonial, Church served as the manager of the new boarding house which operated year-round.

Thousands have passed through its portals over the decades, so it is no wonder that some guests have encountered the supernatural during their stay. The hotel's staff are privy to stories of children playing in the hallway and the sound of bouncing balls in the middle of the night. Some allege the playful spirits haunting the hotel are two children who drowned over a century ago. These anomalies occurred when no children were present at the inn.

During paranormal investigations, ghost hunters recorded electronic voice phenomenon (EVP) in the hotel's lobby. At least one guest heard loud banging on the door to his room only to find no one present when he answered the door. Unexplained expressions are chilling enough but when a photographer overnighted there, he witnessed an arm reach across the bed as if stretching to grab something, according to author Craig McManus.

> *"The sight of a spectral arm will make a deeper impression and convert more people to a belief in their hereafter in ten minutes that a whole regiment of preachers, no matter how eloquent."*
> —Paschal Beverly Randolph. M.D.

Those who experienced the paranormal here say the fourth and fifth floors are the most spirited. Some even encountered the "Lady in Blue." It is surmised that the female apparition is a former chambermaid who carries on her daily routine, although in another dimension.

This writer visited the hotel during the pandemic along with psychic medium Bobbi Torres. For the most part, the grand hotel stood empty of humans but that was not the case with the unseen guests. Bobbi felt the hotel was full to the rafters with spirits who would be happy to hang out a "No Vacancy" sign any day of the week. The souls were extremely pleased to have the place to themselves.

Those who dwell in the afterlife can read thoughts and sense feelings of the living. They hear us, mind-to-mind via energy, not sound waves. The invisible lodgers conveyed they were "thrilled;" they felt like the hotel was "theirs" again. The resident revenants revealed that when overnight guests are present the visitors' energy dominates the space. The spectral energy felt much bigger and more real in the pandemic induced emptiness. The spirits felt pleased to realize that the absence of people expanded their energy—for them, it was like stepping back in time to an earlier era.

Perhaps only those with an intuitive sensitivity can discern that the Inn of Cape May is a high-spirited hotel full of happy, and benign, ghosts.

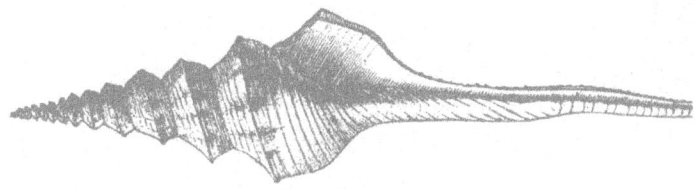

# HOTEL MACOMBER
## 727 BEACH AVENUE

Only three of the great historic hotels, Congress Hotel, the Inn of Cape May (originally called the Colonial Hotel) and the Hotel Macomber stand along Beach Avenue today. The shingle-style Macomber operated as a middle-class lodging when it opened in 1921.

The Macomber is the last historic landmark constructed in the City by the Sea. At the time, the lodge stood as the largest frame structure east of the Mississippi. Among the inn's physical amenities is the sweeping porch offering captivating views of the vast wind-swept beach and surging sea. Today it is home to the Union Park Dining Room restaurant and several spirits.

Hotel Macomber's ephemeral residents rank high among New Jersey's most enduring seaside specters. Room 10 is notoriously haunted. Guests often discern dresser drawers opening and closing. Lights mysteriously turn on and off, as do some of the bathroom fixtures. Some guests sense a presence in the room. Mysteriously, doors slam without benefit of human hand.

Psychic medium Craig McManus unearthed the denizen's identity. Irene Wright was a former guest who frequented the hotel year after year in the 1940s and 50s. Miss Wright adored her Cape May accommodations, so it now appears she refuses to leave. Who can blame her?

Another oft-told tale concerns the postmortem capers of a 1930s-era waitress who choked on a chicken bone when she swiped leftover poultry off a diner's dinner plate. Apparently in a "fowl" mood, one day her spirit shoved a former pastry chef against a shelf in the walk-in refrigerator. The shabby looking specter raised tablecloths and, in the kitchen, moved knives from one place to another when the chef worked alone.

In the dining room, the sound of heavy furniture being dragged is sometimes audible, even though all the rooms are carpeted, and the furnishings are light-weight wicker. The furniture is not actually being moved only the noise of such is evident. This phenomenon is likely a release of spirit energy which manifests as sound.

In the ground level shops, workers report radios turn on without benefit of human hand and tune to Country Western stations.

A former owner, Sarah Davis, committed suicide by shooting herself at the Macomber. Perhaps some of the inexplicable events that transpire here may be Sarah still in residence.

The Hotel Macomber is a great place to launch your supernatural survey of the Jersey Shore.

# CAPE MAY FISH MARKET
## 408 WASHINGTON STREET

When Paula Geserick first entered the building housing the Cape May Fish Market, she felt the structure's special energy. In fact, the restaurant's location on the Washington Street Mall is *extraordinary* because the spot is a hotbed of paranormal activity harboring at least eight (!) ghosts.

Serving as the general manager, Paula enjoys the quiet time after hours when she can catch up with work. Although she feels comfortable being alone in the eatery after closing, the atmosphere felt different one particular night as she stayed to stuff menus. When Paula distinctly felt someone watching her, she surveyed the room and spotted a man who looked a lot like Abraham Lincoln.

So unnerved, she couldn't get out of the building fast enough!

Paula is used to seeing ghosts—she sighted her first apparition at 11-years-old. Nevertheless, she finds being face-to-face with one discomforting (who wouldn't?). She particularly took exception when the same Lincoln-like ghost showed up in her bedroom. That's when she called in ghost buster Craig McManus.

As the psychic medium walked through the restaurant, he sensed the presence of at least eight spirits. He says the location is a gathering place for the undead who have no place else to go. Also, the building may have once functioned as a brothel. This presumption aligns with Paula's sighting of an older, plump woman with gray hair severely styled in a bun. The gray woman exudes an imposing presence and most likely served as the "house mother" or madam.

Full-bodied apparitions are one of the most dramatic manifestations of the afterlife, but they are only the beginning of the goings-on at the Cape May Fish Market according to the South Jersey Ghost Research (SJGR) organization.

There is more to the eatery's supernatural side. One waitress felt an invisible someone pull her pony tail. Others observed decorative prints fall off the wall—one at a time. On one occasion, Paula hung her sweater on a clothes hook and for some reason, looked back at the sweater. Inexplicably the arm stood straight out and then flopped down—as if an unseen hand held it out then let go. This anomaly occurred in front of two other onlookers.

When paranormal investigators surveyed the restaurant, they experienced a male energy in the kitchen who psychics identified as the house steward. Psychic mediums discern his spirit lingers performing chores and preparing meals. Other perceived phantoms are women outfitted in Victorian attire, large hats and long dresses, and men in suits.

The spirits haunting the Cape May Fish Market actively responded to questions asked by investigators via thumping noises and causing the Tri-Field meter to react (the Tri-Field meter is a device that measures electromagnetic fields).

Physical anomalies transpired during SJGR's investigation as well. Two investigators experienced a temperature drop of 8 degrees in less than a minute and one felt something brush up against her right arm. Two investigators reported seeing shadows while investigating the basement. Another heard a voice and what sounded like footsteps coming from the back of the room. Yet another investigator reported the chair next to her moved.

In an attempt to interact with the spirits and gain specific information about the resident entities, investigators ask questions utilizing the REM pod, a device that detects energy disturbances and fluctuations. The occupant spirits here caused the REM to alarm again and again in response to questions posed.

During a particular EVP session utilizing the REM pod, an investigator received the impression of a female spirit with long, blonde hair wearing a blue dress. Investigator Bridget LeConey asked, "Did you have a blue dress?" The REM responded affirmatively. Then, "Do you like the changes happening upstairs?" The REM lit up. "Would you like to see people living there when it's fixed up?" Again, the REM lit up. Another investigator telepathically heard the female entity say, "Yeah, then I could borrow their clothes." Paula laughed remembering the episode with her sweater. Bridget asked, "Do you like Paula's sweaters?" REM immediately lit up.

Some clairvoyants discern a hostile aspect; the structure witnessed its share of sadness, loss and violence. A lot of lingering energy exists throughout the building, but SJGR picked up particularly strong energies in the second and third floor restrooms. Paula herself experienced a disembodied woman in the second floor restroom. The spirits sensed in the lavatories exuded a deep sadness—one due to loss of a loved one, the other over her fate as a prostitute.

Investigators also picked up on both suicide and murder in the building. The violence is associated with nefarious activities occurring within the structure throughout its history. One said, *"...the energy feels residual but there are many layers. I believe the apartments were used as a boarding house for blue collar workers and this eventually degenerated into a low-rent complex filled with drugs, prostitution and gambling. There were constant fights, yelling and violence."*

Although the history of the 1868 building is vague, many different people passed through its portals over the decades. The strong emotions associated with decadent living created a lasting impression on 408 Washington Street that manifests to this day.

# EMLEN PHYSICK ESTATE
## 1048 WASHINGTON STREET

The Mid-Atlantic Center for the Arts (MAC) is headquartered in a truly haunted mansion at 1048 Washington Street. The historically minded group saved the old manse from demolition in the 1970s.

Built in 1879 for Dr. Emlen Physick, his mother, Frances Ralsten and his aunts, Isabella and Emilie Parmentier, eccentric Philadelphia architect Frank Furness designed the stick-style, 18-room showplace.

The hauntings date to the mid-1940s when the residents were afraid to live in the house because of its ghostly inhabitants. The family heard footsteps and noises every night and eventually gave up searching for the cause because it proved futile.

Psychic medium Craig McManus has written three books about Cape May's hauntings, documenting spirit activity at dozens of properties. His investigations at the Physick Estate unearthed several spectral residents.

The most active wraith is Aunt Emilie who stays behind to watch over the house. Although the doctor's mother successfully crossed over, her spirit remains in the house as residual energy, especially in her bedroom according to McManus.

Another resident he identified is Isabelle, or Bella, Mrs. Ralston's invalid younger sister, who died in 1883, shortly after the family moved into the mansion.

The Carriage House is spirited by one of the servants, possibly a groomsman or driver. Several MAC staffers, whose offices are on the building's second floor, have heard the wraith of the resident servant. Once his specter appeared in the dead of winter walking up to the entrance and into the building wrote McManus in *Ghosts of Cape May*.

MAC runs various ghost tours of the house year-around and attendees often encounter aspects of the paranormal first-hand. Experience your own ghost adventure up close and personal!

# CAPE MAY POINT
## WORLD WAR II BUNKER
CAPE MAY STATE PARK

During the Second World War, enemy submarines infiltrated New Jersey's coastal waters. To protect the shoreline, the US Army Corps of Engineers constructed the cement gun emplacement bunker standing east of the Cape May Lighthouse in Cape May Point State Park. The Cape May fortification worked in tandem with batteries at Lewes, Delaware to control the entrance to Delaware Bay from enemy ships.

Naval gunnery crews manned the site and spent hours scanning the horizon for enemy ships and submarines. In fact, a German U-Boat commander surrendered his vessel off Cape May's coast at the end of the war.

Equipped like any other fort, men stationed inside the underground battery #223, stopped foreign U-boats from entering NJ waters. Concealed with sand, sod and sea grass, the camouflaged, cement hulk, at the time, stood on dry land. Time and tides eroded the camouflage and exposed the hideaway. Time, and perhaps its close proximity to water, revealed spectral sailors still living inside the concrete haunt, their ghostly faces sometimes peering out the gun ports and astonishing unsuspecting visitors.

When open to the public the bunker became the site of uncanny encounters. Visitors witnessed spectral sailors performing their duty inside and outside the edifice. Eerie conversations were discerned, but could not be deciphered. Lighters flared as ethereal guardsmen lit their cigarettes.

These men, so devoted to duty, remained on guard long after they passed away.

## CAPE MAY LIGHTHOUSE
### 215 LIGHTHOUSE AVENUE

In the dark of night, it's easy to imagine the comfort a lighthouse beam brought to generations of sailors. To this day, the beacon remains, lighting the way.

Some fishermen and early morning joggers encountered mysterious ramblers along the beach and at the Cape May Point Light. The visitors think they see kindred souls taking a sunrise stroll when in fact, these others are detached and non-responsive, because they exist in another dimension, an "other" world of their own.

The lighthouse structure was completed in 1859, and its first-order Fresnel lens illuminated the night sky for the first time on Halloween night that same year. (That lens is on display at the Cape May County Museum.) The present light is the third lighthouse on the site. Today, the U.S. Coast Guard maintains the lighthouse; and the Mid-Atlantic Center for the Arts (MAC), leases the property from the state and operates the historic site.

For over one hundred years, visitors to Cape May ventured to the Point and climbed the 199 spiraling stairs to catch a dizzying view of the seaside from a seagull's perspective.

There are those who deny the existence of otherworldly inhabitants perambulating about the light, but those who have witnessed the ghostly goings on swear that spirits swarm about the antique light.

One tale told by Craig McManus on MAC's "Ghosts in the Lighthouse Trolley Tour" concerns a spectral woman spotted on the spiral staircase. She holds a lantern in one hand, and a child in the other. Appearing in a flowing, white gown, the female spirit seems tethered to the light's first landing.

Among legends, the woman in white is a female ghost dressed in white, and associated with a local tragedy. Common to these ghostly tales are accidental death, murder/suicide, and the themes of loss, betrayal, and unrequited love.

# ACKNOWLEDGEMENTS

I want to express an ocean of gratitude to Charles J. Adams III; Boni Bates, Garden State Ghost Hunters; Clay Borneman, Cumberland County Paranormal; Sandy Epstein, Guggenheim Library; Pamela Garber; Paula Geserick, Cape May Fish Market; the late Hans Holzer; Dave Juliano and Bridget LeConey, South Jersey Ghost Research; the late John Bailey Lloyd; Point Pleasant Historical Society; Bobbi Apostolou Torres for sharing her Spirit insights and her spirited home; & Debra Tremper, Graphic Designer, Six Penny Graphics for contributing to *Ghosts of the Jersey Shore*. I thank all my readers, and the booksellers and librarians who keep them supplied, from the bottom of my heart.

# BIBLIOGRAPHY

Adams, Charles J., III. *Cape May Ghost Stories, Book Two.* Exeter House Books, 1996.

_____. *Atlantic County Ghost Stories.* Exeter House Books, 2003.

Bergstein, San. "Haunted NJ: Cape May's Ghostly Hotspots." October 24, 2015, https://bestofnj.com/features/holidays/halloween/haunted-nj-cape-mays-ghostly-hotspots.

Bremner, Barbara. "Ghosts of the Jersey Shore." October 14, 2015. https://bestofnj.com/haunting-the-jersey-shore.

"Cape May, NJ." *Haunted Towns.* Season 1, Episode 7. Destination America Channel, 2017.

Chesek, Tom, "Ghosts In The House 'Turn of the Screw' at Monmouth U." *Asbury Park Press,* June 18, 2004.

Considine, Bob. "Dark Shadows at the Shore." *Asbury Park Press,* October 25, 2008.

Donnelly, Mark and Diehl, Daniel. *Pirates of New Jersey.* Stackpole Books, 2010.

*Fact or Faked, Paranormal Files* (Syfy channel). "Bay Area Hysteria/Jersey Shore Haunting." Season 2, Episode 14, April 24, 2012.

Fryckstaedt, Olav W., Ed. *Stephen Crane: Uncollected Writings.* Upsala Press, 1963.

"Ghosts at the Physick Estate." Retrieved from: http://www.capemaymac.org/attractions/emlenphysickestate.html

Hauck, Dennis William. *Haunted Places, The National Directory*. Penguin Books, 1996.

Hawk, Tim. "The living—and the dead—love Cape May." NJ Advance Media for NJ.com. https://www.nj.com/cape-may-county/2018/10/haunted_cape_may.html.

Heston, Alfred M. *Absegami: Annals of Eyren Haven and Atlantic City, 1609-1904*. Higginson Book Company, 1997 (reprint).

Hopkins, Amanda. "Spirits Lingers at Resorts." *Atlantic City Weekly*, October 24, 2012.

Kopp, Jennifer Brownstone. "Spirited Cape May: More Than Meets the Eye." *Cape May Star & Wave*, October 1, 2000.

_____. "Spirited Cape May: Do You Believe?" *Cape May Star & Wave*, October 2, 2000.

Lloyd, John Bailey. *Eighteen Miles of History on Long Beach Island*. Down the Shore Publishing, 1986.

_____. *Two Centuries of History on Long Beach Island*. Down the Shore Publishing, 2005.

Kelly, Kathy A. *Asbury Park's Ghosts and Legends*. Paranormal Books & Curiosities Publishing, 2010.

Kimmel, Richard J. and Timper, Karen E. *Folklore of the Jersey Shore*. Schiffer Books, 2012.

Macken, Lynda Lee. *Ghosts of the Jersey Shore*, First Edition. Black Cat Press, 2011.

_____. *Haunted Long Beach Island*. Black Cat Press, 2013.

_____. *Ghosts of the Jersey Shore II*. Black Cat Press, 2014.

_____. *Haunted Monmouth County*. Black Cat Press, 2014.

_____. *Haunted Houses of New Jersey*. Black Cat Press, 2016.

_____. *Haunted Cape May*. Black Cat Press, 2020.

Marhoefer, Laurie. "Ghost Stories at the Surflight Theater." *The Press of Atlantic City*, October 25, 2001.

McManus, Craig. *The Ghosts of Cape May.* ChannelCraig, Inc., 2005.

_____. "Ghosts of Cape May Trolley Tour." The Mid-Atlantic Center for the Arts. October 27, 2012.

O'Neill, Maggie. *Into the Mystic Legend and Ghost Tour.* August 8, 2012.

Perrotto, Patrick and Tom Hanley. *Shadows of Shadow Lawn* (DVD). Hawk TV, 2005.

Reeser, A. L. *Ghost Stories of Atlantic City and Other Odd and Ghastly Tales from the World's Playground.* 1stSight Press, 2010.

Reeser, Tim. *Ghost Stories of Ocean City, NJ.* Ghostlore, Inc., 2003

Reynolds, Joe. "Sandy Hook is a Weird & Creepy Park." *Atlantic Highlands Herald,* November 9, 2009.

Roberts, Russell and Richard Youmans, *Down the Jersey Shore.* Rutgers University Press, 1993.

Roncace, Kelly. "The Haunted Jersey Shore." May 15, 2019. https://www.nj.com/entertainment/2017/07/8_jersey_shore_haunts_to_explore_after_the_sun_set.html

Shad, Jacob Jr. "Spooky Night at the Wildwood Museum." Shore News Today, July 7, 2011.

Siebold, Daniel and Charles J. Adams III. *Legends of Long Beach Island.* Exeter House Books, 1985.

_____. *Cape May Ghost Stories.* Exeter House Books, 1988.

Stansfield, Charles A., Jr. *Haunted Jersey Shore.* Stackpole Books, 2006.

Sudol, Karen & Moore, Kirk. "Jersey Shore Haunts." *Asbury Park Press,* October 3, 2006.

Suit, Lauren. "J. Thompson Baker house a 'hot spot' for paranormal investigators." *Shore News Today,* December 14, 2011.

Tempera, Jackie. "Tap into the supernatural on LBI." *Asbury Park Press,* August 24, 2012.

Tischler, Susan. "Long Gone but Refusing to Leave: The Ghosts of Cape May." http://www.capemay.com/blog/2002/10/long-gone-but-refusing-to-leave-the-ghosts-of-cape-may/#sthash.9KcO7JeO.dpuf.

———. "The Dead of Winter." http://www.capemay.com/blog/2010/03/the-dead-of-winter/.

———. "Favorite Cape May Haunts." http://www.capemay.com/Editorial/october06/favoritehaunts.html.

———. "Ghost of the Lighthouse." http://www.capemay.com/Editorial/october07/lighthouseghosts.html.

Urgo, Jacqueline L. "Tapping into the Spirit of Cape May." *Philadelphia Inquirer*, February 29, 1996.

Wright, Jack. *Tommy's Folly: Through Fires, Hurricanes and War, the Story of Congress Hall, Cape May, America's Oldest Seaside Hotel*. Beach Plum Press, 2003.

# WEBSITES

Absecon Lighthouse: www.abseconlighthouse.org

Asbury Radio: www.asburyradio.com

City of Cape May: www.capemaycity.com

Craig McManus, Psychic Medium: www.craigmcmanus.com

Cumberland County Paranormal: www.cumberlandcountyparanormal.com

Early History of West Long Branch: www.westlongbranch.org

Garden State Ghost Hunters: www.gardenstateghosthunters.com

Haunted New Jersey: www.hauntednewjersey.com

Hereford Inlet Lighthouse: www.herefordlighthouse.org

Inn of Cape May: www.innofcapemay.com

Lighthouse Friends: lightousefriends.com

Lucy the Elephant: www.lucytheelephant.org

Mid-Atlantic Center for the Arts & Humanities: www.capemaymac.org

New Jersey Ghost Hunters Society: www.njghs.net

New Jersey History's Mysteries: www.njhm.com

Psychic Jane Doherty: www.janedoherty.com

Resorts Casino Hotel: www.resortsac.com/history

South Jersey Ghost Research: www.southjerseyghostresearch.org

South Jersey Paranormal Research: www.sjpr.org

Stephen Crane House: www.thestephencranehouse.org

Surflight Theater: www.surflight.org

Wikipedia: www.wikipedia.org

# OTHER BOOKS BY LYNDA LEE MACKEN

Adirondack Ghosts
Adirondack Ghosts II
Adirondack Ghosts III
Adirondack Ghosts Road Trip
Array of Hope, An Afterlife Journal
Catskill Ghosts
Empire Ghosts, Historic Haunts in New York State
Ghost Hunting the Mohawk Valley
Ghosts of the Jersey Shore
Ghosts of the Jersey Shore II
Haunted Cape May
Haunted Hamptons
Haunted History of Staten Island
Haunted Houses of New Jersey
Haunted Houses of the Hudson Valley
Haunted Lake George
Haunted Lake Placid
Haunted Long Beach Island
Haunted Long Island II
Haunted Monmouth County
Haunted New Hope
Haunted Outer Banks
Haunted Salem & Beyond

# More Coastal Ghost Stories

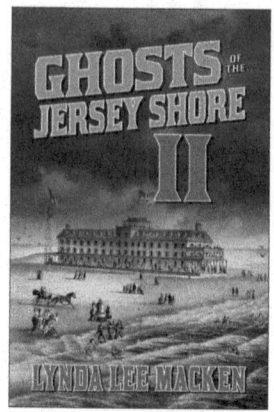

## Read More About Spirited Seasides